YOUR GROWLING GUTS

and

DYNAMIC

Digestive System

FIND OUT HOW YOUR BODY WORKS!

Paul Mason

Crabtree Publishing Company

www.crabtreebooks.com

Crabtree Publishing Company
www.crabtreebooks.com
1-800-387-7650

Published in Canada
Crabtree Publishing
616 Welland Avenue
St. Catharines, ON
L2M 5V6

Published in the United States
Crabtree Publishing
PMB 59051
350 Fifth Ave, 59th Floor
New York, NY 10118

Author: Paul Mason
Editorial director: Kathy Middleton
Editors: Annabel Stones, Shirley Duke, Kelly Spence
Designer: Rocket Design (East Anglia) Ltd
Consultant: John Clancy, Former Senior
    Lecturer in Applied Human Physiology
Proofreaders: Susie Brooks, Rebecca Sjonger
Prepress technician: Margaret Amy Salter
Print and production coordinator: Margaret Amy Salter

Published by Crabtree Publishing Company in 2016

Printed in the USA/082015/SN20150529

Picture credits:
Getty Images: p22 bl LTL/ Contributor; iStockphoto: p5cl, p7 bl, p13 cr; Science Photo Library: p3 ct, p13 tl CNRI, p19 cr BO VEISLAND, MI&I, p19 br GASTROLAB, p20 bl CNRI, p21 tr LUNAGRAFIX, p26 ANIMATE4.COM; Shutterstock: p3 t, p3 cb, p3 b, p4, p5 r, p5 br, p7 t, p7 cr, p7 br, p8 bc, p9 br, p11 t, p11 bl, p11 br, p13 tr, p14, p15 bl, p16, p17 t, p17 br, p18, p19 tr, p21 cl, p21 bl, p21 cr, p22 br, p25 tr, p25 bl, p25 bc, p25 br, p27 br, p28 cl, p28 br, p29 all; Wellcome Library, London CC Wikimedia Commons: p9 cr.
Graphic elements from Shutterstock.

Artwork: Ian Thompson: p10, p12; Ian Thompson/Stefan Chabluk p8 tr; Stefan Chabluk: p6, p9 tl, p15 tr, p23 br, p24, p27 t.

Every effort has been made to clear copyright. Should there be any inadvertent omission, please apply to the publisher for rectification.

The website addresses (URLs) included in this book were valid at the time of going to press. However, it is possible that contents or addresses may have changed since the publication of this book. No responsibility for any such changes can be accepted by either the author or the Publisher.

Library and Archives Canada Cataloguing in Publication

Mason, Paul, 1967-, author
    Your growling guts and dynamic digestive system / Paul Mason.

(Your brilliant body!)
Includes index.
Issued in print and electronic formats.
ISBN 978-0-7787-2197-0 (bound).--ISBN 978-0-7787-2211-3 (paperback).--
ISBN 978-1-4271-1708-3 (pdf).--ISBN 978-1-4271-1702-1 (html)

    1. Digestive organs--Juvenile literature. I. Title.

QM301.M37 2015   j612.3   C2015-903170-2
                                        C2015-903171-0

Library of Congress Cataloging-in-Publication Data

Mason, Paul, 1967-
 Your growling guts and dynamic digestive system / Paul Mason.
    pages cm. -- (Your brilliant body!)
 Includes index.
 ISBN 978-0-7787-2197-0 (reinforced library binding : alk. paper) --
ISBN 978-0-7787-2211-3 (pbk. : alk. paper) --
ISBN 978-1-4271-1708-3 (electronic pdf : alk. paper) --
ISBN 978-1-4271-1702-1 (electronic html : alk. paper)
1. Gastrointestinal system--Juvenile literature. I. Title.

QP151.M34 2016
612.3'2--dc23
                            2015015362

CONTENTS

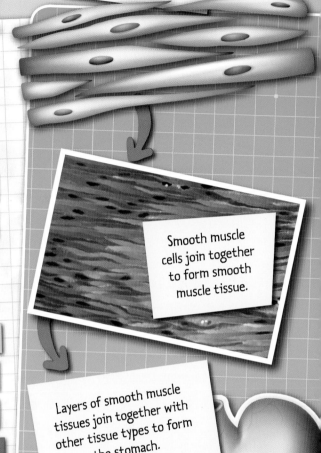

All living things are made of tiny building blocks called cells. These are smooth muscle cells.

Smooth muscle cells join together to form smooth muscle tissue.

Layers of smooth muscle tissues join together with other tissue types to form the stomach.

The stomach is a large organ in your digestive system. As food passes through this system, nutrients are taken out for your body to use.

YOUR GROWLING GUTS

Did you realize that you are basically hollow? There's a tube running RIGHT THROUGH your body! It starts in your mouth and finishes at your bottom. The tube is your digestive system. Foods and drinks go in one end, and something much less pleasant comes out of the other!

Is it really just a tube?

Not really, no. When you started life it was a tube. But as your body grew, your digestive system became more complicated. It developed muscular walls for moving food downward. It widened in places, to form your stomach and large intestine. Little **valves** appeared, to stop food from traveling the wrong way through the system. It also developed loops of tube that link to your **circulatory system**.

What is a digestive system for?

Your digestive system takes **nutrients** from food and passes them on to your circulatory system for distribution to cells around the body. These nutrients are used for energy, movement, growth, and repair of damaged parts. Having gotten as much useful material as possible from your food, your digestive system also gets rid of anything that isn't needed.

STRANGE BUT TRUE!

An average person from a wealthy country eats roughly 110,231 pounds (50 tons) of food (that's 25 adult white rhinos!) during his or her lifetime. He or she also drinks about 13,208 gallons (50,000 L) of fluid.

How does it work?

The first stage of digestion is for food to be broken into smaller pieces, which can move more easily through the body. (If you've ever swallowed a too-big mouthful, you'll know why this is a good idea.) This process is called **mechanical digestion**.

At the same time as your food is broken into smaller pieces, **chemical digestion** starts. Chemicals called **enzymes** speed up the breakdown of food into smaller and smaller parts. Finally, the nutrients from food are small enough to pass into the blood.

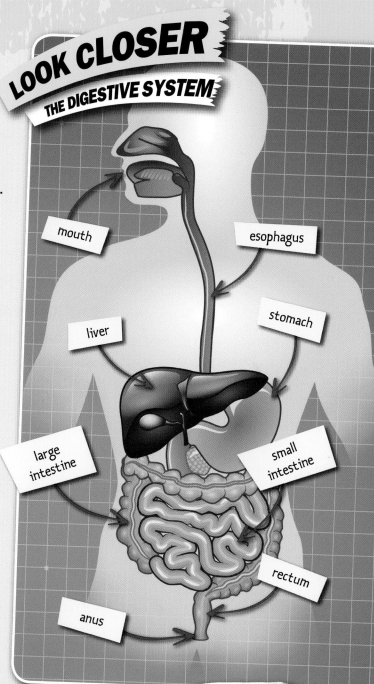

mouth

esophagus

liver

stomach

large intestine

small intestine

rectum

anus

Digestion begins in your mouth, when you chew food.

DID YOU KNOW?

Thin people don't have smaller stomachs.

There is no relation between how thin you are and the size of your stomach. Everyone's stomach is around the size of a fist and stretches depending on what is put into it.

See for yourself

How much can a stomach hold?

Find a half-gallon (2 L) bottle. This holds the same volume as a completely full adult stomach. Now put five tablespoons of water into the bottle. This is about 75 millileters—which is the average volume of a completely empty stomach.

THE MIRACULOUS MOUTH

Your mouth is the gateway to your digestive system. Mind you, the guests don't get a very friendly welcome. They're smashed up by your teeth and swirled around in saliva, before being swallowed down a dark hole. It's fortunate they are only bits of food!

Rough guide to the mouth

You may not think much about your mouth—but there's actually a lot going on inside it. A thin bony plate called the **hard palate** separates the mouth from the **nasal passages**. The **soft palate** is flexible and is important for swallowing and breathing. Lips are important for all kinds of things, including speech, allowing food into your mouth, and keeping it there while you're chewing.

LOOK CLOSER
MOUTH PARTS

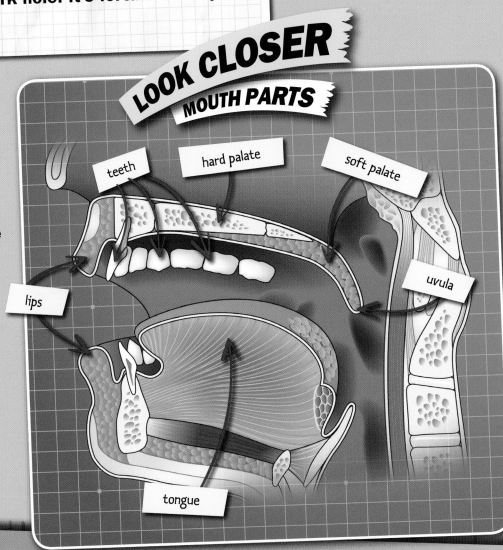

- teeth
- hard palate
- soft palate
- lips
- uvula
- tongue

A close-up of the surface of the tongue.

The tongue

The tongue is an organ made mainly of muscle. Along with the cheeks and lips, it is used to control food while chewing and keeps food in place so that it can be ground up by the teeth. The tongue is coated with a **mucus membrane** (a layer of slimy material), which helps stop **microbes** from entering the body.

The mouth and taste

Scientists say there are four basic tastes: sweet, salty, sour, and bitter. Your tongue is covered with nerve endings called **taste buds**. Together, the taste buds send a message to your brain about what you are eating. They also sense the temperature of food and its texture.

Hotel Bacteria

An ordinary mouth contains well over 50 different types of **bacteria**. In total, there can easily be more bacteria in someone's mouth than there are people on Earth (which is seven billion and rising). Some bacteria are harmful; others are helpful.

The average mouth also contains over 70 types of fungus, and a few **viruses** and parasites. Yuck!

Just a few of the billions of bacteria on someone's tongue.

No one is really sure what it's for, but touching the **uvula** makes you gag. It may also be important in speech and the swallowing process.

STRANGE BUT TRUE!

Scientists once thought that the ability to roll your tongue into a tube shape was inherited from your parents. This may not be 100% true. In one study, half of a group of children could tongue-roll at six or seven. By the time they were 12, three-quarters could do it. They had learned to tongue roll!

See for yourself

As well as being used when eating, your tongue is crucial for speech. Moving it around in your mouth makes it possible to form words. Testing this is simple. Just try speaking normally, but with your tongue deliberately kept pressed against the bottom of your mouth, against your lower teeth.

CHEW ON THIS

canines

molars

premolars

incisors

Teeth start the process of breaking food down by mashing it up as you chew. Teeth are also important for speaking—try talking without your tongue touching your teeth and you'll see!

How many teeth do you have?

In total, most people have 52 teeth in their lifetime. Not all at once, though! There wouldn't be room in your mouth.

Stage 1 Young children have 20 teeth by the time they are about three years old. These are called **baby teeth**, or primary teeth.

Stage 2 New teeth, growing behind, start pushing the baby teeth out when you are about six years old. By the age of 12, most children have 28 new teeth.

Stage 3 In their 20s, most people get four more teeth, called **wisdom teeth**. So adults with all their teeth have 32 in total.

Are all teeth the same?

No—and each type of tooth in your mouth has a specific job to do. At the front of your mouth you have **incisors** and **canines**. These are used for biting into things, from apples to burgers. The incisors slice into food, while canines grip and tear. Further back in your mouth are **premolars** and **molars**, which are used for chewing. This breaks your food down into pieces small enough to be swallowed.

STRANGE BUT TRUE!

No two people have exactly the same teeth. The marks left behind when you bite something are as unique as fingerprints. Some criminals have even been identified from their bite marks!

LOOK CLOSER
A TOOTH

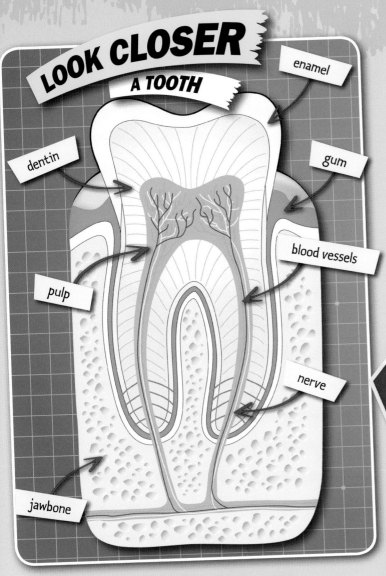

- enamel
- dentin
- gum
- blood vessels
- pulp
- nerve
- jawbone

Your mouth waters for a reason.

Saliva does an important job in digestion. It mixes with food in your mouth, helping to break it down. It also acts as a **lubricant**, allowing the food to slide down your throat when you swallow.

Saliva also washes the chemicals in food into your taste buds. Without saliva, you wouldn't be able to taste what you are eating.

DON'T TRY THIS AT HOME!

In the past, people with a toothache often visited a barber to have the painful tooth removed (there were no trained dentists back then).

One way to remove a tooth was with a tooth key. The "key" end was placed over the tooth, the "handle" was turned, and with luck, the tooth popped out. If you were unlucky, the tooth shattered and the pieces had to be individually pulled out from your bleeding jaw.

What are teeth made of?

Teeth are not hard all the way through. Under the hard outer crust that you see when someone smiles, there are several more layers. **Enamel**—on the outside—is the hardest tissue in the body. A softer layer called **dentin** sits under the enamel and is the second line of protection if the enamel cracks. The hard outer layers protect the **pulp**—this is full of nerve endings and **blood vessels** and is VERY painful if touched!

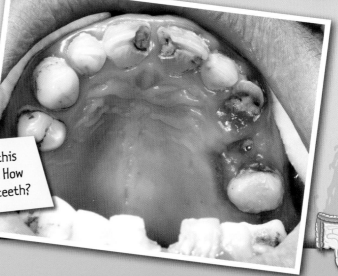

The bacteria that cause tooth decay like this double in number every four to five hours. How often do you think you need to clean your teeth?

JOURNEY DOWN THE ESOPHAGUS

The **esophagus** is sometimes called the "food pipe." It is a muscular tube that passes food from your mouth to your stomach. The esophagus works a bit like a snake swallowing its prey!

The art of swallowing

Once your teeth, tongue, and saliva have gotten your food to just the right consistency, it forms into a little ball, or **bolus**. You don't have to think about this, it just happens.

The bolus gets pushed to the back of your mouth and is swallowed down the esophagus. The esophagus's muscular walls expand ahead of the bolus and **contract** behind it, forcing food down. This muscle action is called **peristalsis**. Food always moves in just one direction—which makes it possible to drink a glass of water while standing on your head.

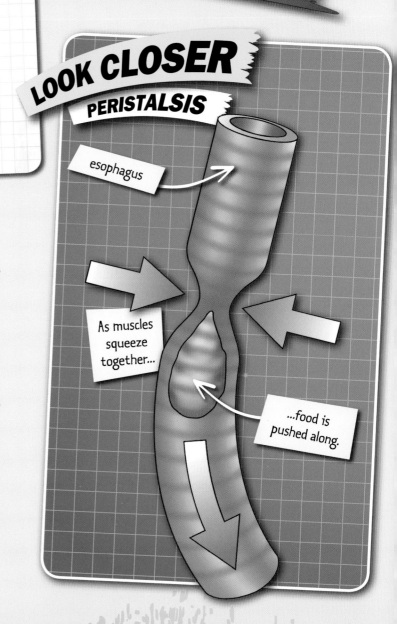

LOOK CLOSER
PERISTALSIS

esophagus

As muscles squeeze together...

...food is pushed along.

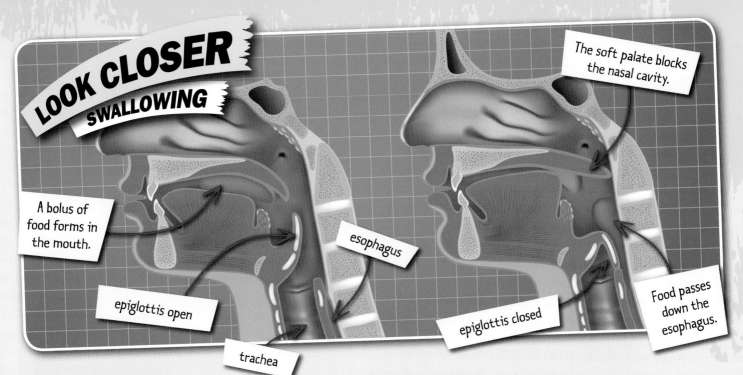

The soft palate blocks the nasal cavity.

A bolus of food forms in the mouth.

esophagus

epiglottis open

trachea

epiglottis closed

Food passes down the esophagus.

The epiglottis

The esophagus shares your mouth's rear exit with another tube, called the **trachea** (or windpipe), which leads down to your lungs. When you swallow, a flap called the **epiglottis** covers the trachea's opening. This stops food from entering your trachea and blocking it, or even getting into your lungs.

Usually, the epiglottis does its job perfectly—but food can sometimes get trapped in someone's windpipe. This blocks the airway and stops air from getting to the lungs. If the food is stuck for more than a few seconds, the person could suffocate.

DO TRY THIS AT HOME –

but only in an emergency!

If someone gets something stuck in his or her windpipe, the blockage needs to be removed as quickly as possible. Call loudly for help from an adult.

If the person is over the age of one, get him or her to lean forward onto your hand. Use your other hand to strike them on the back, between the shoulder blades, using the heel of your hand. Do this up to five times—it may loosen the blockage.

STRANGE BUT TRUE!

Esophagogastroscopy is a procedure that involves looking at the inside of the esophagus and stomach. The first esophagogastroscopy was almost certainly performed in 1868, when a curious German doctor named Adolf Kussmaul examined a professional sword swallower.

THE BODY'S FOOD MIXER

Once it has been swallowed, food is squeezed all the way down the esophagus and into the stomach. This is like a stretchy bag of muscle. Here, mechanical digestion AND chemical digestion take place.

The food churner

Your stomach works like a cement mixer for your digestive system. Well, a food mixer, at least. It takes delivery of lightly chewed boluses of food from your mouth. Then the muscles that make up the stomach start contracting and relaxing, churning up the food.

This contracting and expanding to churn up food is normally just a background noise. Once in a while, though, it can be heard! The rumbling is particularly loud when you're hungry, and the churning noise echoes around inside your empty stomach.

LOOK CLOSER
STOMACH

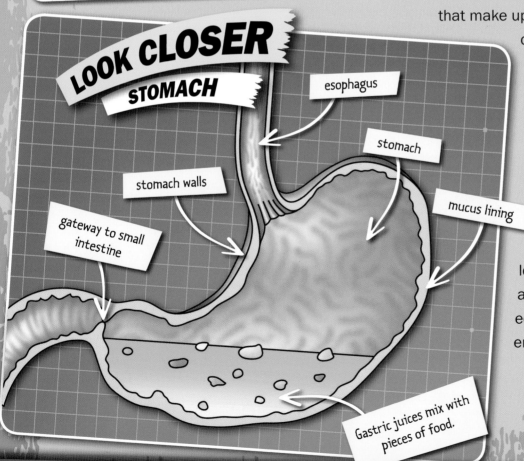

esophagus

stomach

stomach walls

mucus lining

gateway to small intestine

Gastric juices mix with pieces of food.

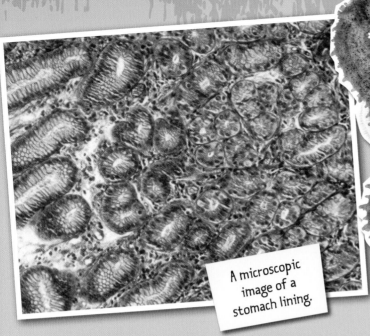

A microscopic image of a stomach lining.

Acid attack! (on your food)

At the same time as it is churning food, your stomach releases acid, which helps enzymes further break down the chewed-and-churned food. The acid is similar to **hydrochloric acid** that's used to strip rust and paint off metal. It can eat through skin, bone, and just about anything else you might swallow.

All that stomach acid helps to defend your body against some harmful bacteria, which get destroyed. But the stomach also has to defend ITSELF against the acid. It does this by producing a thick mucus lining. When the acid eats the lining away, the stomach just produces more. In the end, your stomach gets a new lining every two weeks or so.

DON'T TRY THIS AT HOME!

In 1822, a Canadian fur trapper named Alexis St. Martin was accidentally shot in the side. The wound healed, but left a hole that went through to his stomach. St. Martin's doctor, William Beaumont, saw this as a great opportunity to study digestion. He spent the next few months dangling bits of food into the patient's stomach on a piece of string, to see what happened to it.

St. Martin died in 1880, at the age of 86—still with a hole in his side.

DID YOU KNOW?

If you stop eating, your stomach doesn't shrink.

Your stomach does shrink down when not in use, but as soon as some food arrives to be processed, it expands again.

THE (LONG) SMALL INTESTINE

BRILLIANT BODY FACT

The small intestine is just about one inch (2.5 cm) across—unless it has been stretched by some food!

When food leaves your stomach, it enters the small intestine. It might be CALLED the small intestine—but an adult's is about 19.5 feet (6 m) long. That's over half the height of the highest diving board in the Olympics!

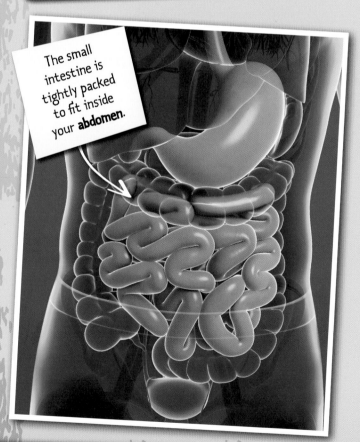

The small intestine is tightly packed to fit inside your **abdomen**.

Why does the small intestine need to be so big?

The small intestine is big because this is where the most important part of the digestion process happens. Here, your body removes about 90% of the nutrients from food. The nutrients are transfered to your blood, ready for delivery to cells around the body. To achieve this, the intestine has three separate areas:

The first part is the duodenum. This connects to the stomach. Here, chemicals containing enzymes mix with the food and break it down into small pieces.

The jejunum is the middle part of the small intestine, which continues the breakdown of food into its individual nutrients.

The ilium is the last part and connects to the large intestine. It is very similar to the jejunum, and this is where the final nutrients are **absorbed** into the blood.

How do nutrients get into the blood?

The small intestine is lined with tiny structures called **villi**, which stick out into the tube of the intestine. Most villi are roughly 0.04 inches (1 mm) long, and have even smaller microvilli sticking out from them. Inside the villi are blood vessels.

In the duodenum and jejunum, the villi are leaf-shaped. They help to release chemicals containing enzymes that break food into its individual nutrients. In the ilium, the villi are finger-like to increase surface area. Here the individual nutrients are absorbed through the walls of the villi into the blood.

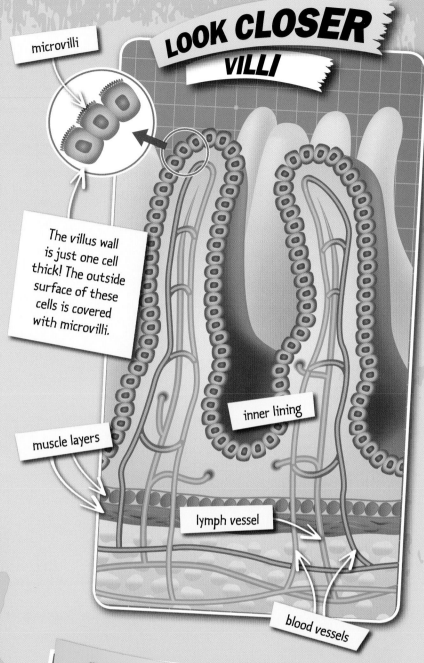

LOOK CLOSER
VILLI

microvilli

The villus wall is just one cell thick! The outside surface of these cells is covered with microvilli.

muscle layers

inner lining

lymph vessel

blood vessels

DID YOU KNOW?

How long does it take?

Food usually stays in the small intestine for one to four hours. After that, most of the nutrients have been absorbed and the remaining food components move down to the large intestine. They can hang out there for 18 hours or longer.

A magnified section of the small intestine shows the inner lining.

STRANGE BUT TRUE!

The small intestine may be long, but it is very thin at just one inch (2.5 cm) in diameter. If it were completely smooth inside, the small intestine's surface area would be about the same as the seat of a chair. The inside of an adult's small intestine has at least the same surface area as your living room!

YOUR LOVELY LIVER

Your small intestine does not do its digestive work alone. A whole team of other organs helps the intestine to work (though these organs are usually counted as separate from the digestive system).

is **bile**, which your duodenum needs in order to break down fat. The bile is stored in your gallbladder ready to be released when needed.

The liver and gallbladder

When blood leaves your small intestine, it contains nutrients. The blood travels straight to the liver. The liver is a bit like a food warehouse, where nutrients are released from the blood and processed. It filters out harmful substances, stores energy, and distributes nutrients to cells around the body.

Your liver also produces chemicals that are used in digestion. One of these

LOOK CLOSER
DIGESTIVE ORGANS

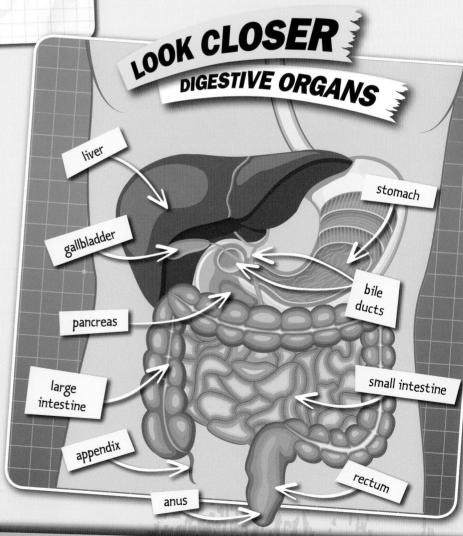

liver

stomach

gallbladder

bile ducts

pancreas

large intestine

small intestine

appendix

rectum

anus

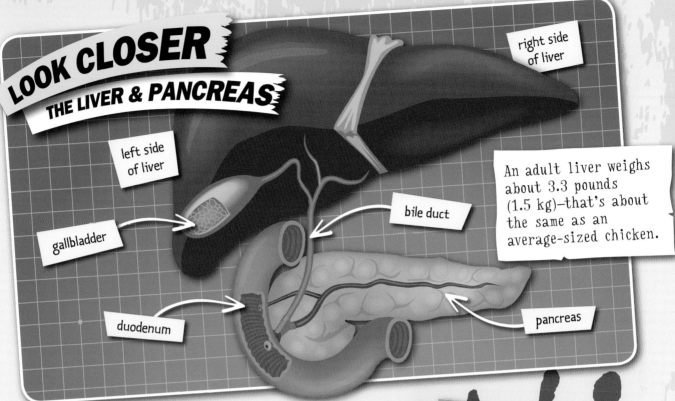

LOOK CLOSER
THE LIVER & PANCREAS

right side of liver

left side of liver

bile duct

gallbladder

An adult liver weighs about 3.3 pounds (1.5 kg)—that's about the same as an average-sized chicken.

duodenum

pancreas

The pancreas

The pancreas's main job is to release enzymes into the duodenum. When food arrives in your duodenum, it has been smashed up in the mouth and churned around in the stomach. But (as anyone who has ever vomited will know) food in your stomach is not 100% liquid. So the enzymes break the food down even more so that nutrients can be absorbed into the blood.

Regrowing a liver

Your liver has an amazing talent—it can grow back. This means that part of a person's liver can be donated to someone else. A section is removed and transplanted into another person. The donor's liver grows back to almost the same size as before.

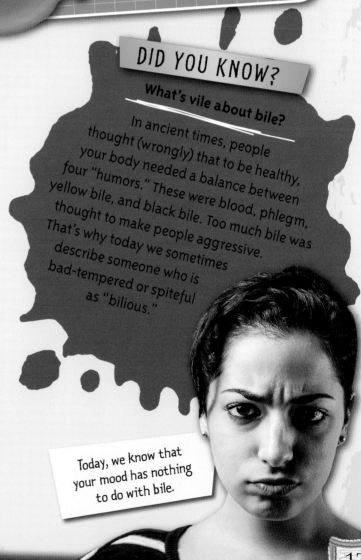

DID YOU KNOW?

What's vile about bile?

In ancient times, people thought (wrongly) that to be healthy, your body needed a balance between four "humors." These were blood, phlegm, yellow bile, and black bile. Too much bile was thought to make people aggressive. That's why today we sometimes describe someone who is bad-tempered or spiteful as "bilious."

Today, we know that your mood has nothing to do with bile.

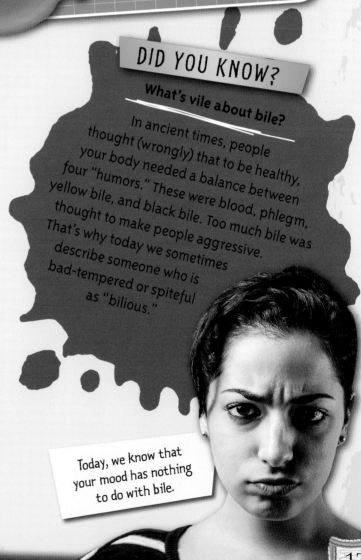

17

THE LARGE INTESTINE

Remember how the small intestine was about 19.5 feet (6 m) long? How big do you think the **LARGE** intestine is? Well, it's actually only about a quarter as long, at about five feet (1.5 m). It can stretch much wider than the small intestine, though, which is how it gets its name.

From liquid to solid

When food leaves the small intestine, it no longer looks anything like food. It is a kind of sloppy liquid. The liquid goes through a valve of muscle that closes tightly behind it. There is no going back now—the valve will not allow it. The liquid has entered the large intestine, where water and the last few nutrients will be removed.

As food passes down the large intestine, the body absorbs its liquid. The food sludge gradually becomes thicker and more solid. Eventually it solidifies into **stool**. This isn't the kind of stool you want to sit on, though—it's another word for

LOOK CLOSER
LARGE INTESTINE

The main part of the large intestine is sometimes called the **colon**.

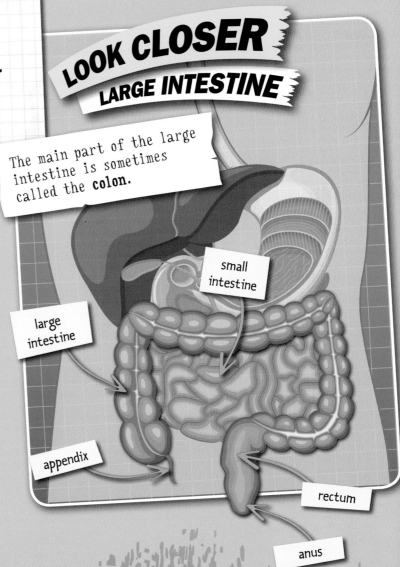

large intestine

small intestine

appendix

rectum

anus

18

feces, or poop. The stool passes into the rectum and finally pass out of your **anus** when you go to the restroom.

Microscopic helpers

Living inside your intestines is a crowd of microscopic helpers called bacteria. In your large intestine, one of the jobs of these microscopic helpers is to break down any undigested food. They also attack any harmful bacteria that have managed to get this far, and even help train your body to fight off disease. The only bad thing about them is that they do produce gas—find out more on the next page...

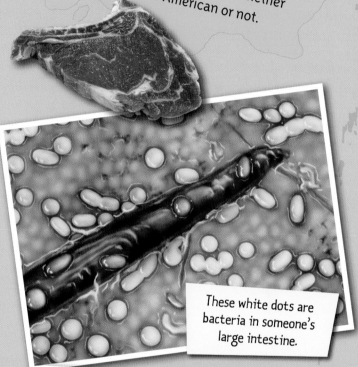

These white dots are bacteria in someone's large intestine.

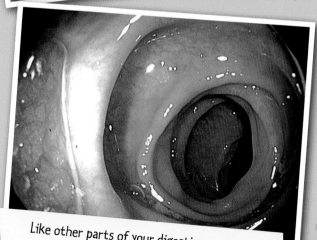

Like other parts of your digestive system, the large intestine is lined with muscles that contract to move food through.

DIGESTIVE WIND

There are over 700 different kinds of bacteria in your large intestine. In total, your guts contain roughly 100 trillion (100,000,000,000,000) microscopic bacteria. That's more or less TEN TIMES the number of cells that make up your whole body!

Bacterial jobs

Each type of bacteria has a job, and many produce things your body needs. The most important are useful **vitamins**. Bacteria also break down **fiber**—hard-to-digest plant matter. While doing their work, the bacteria make **by-products** that the body needs to get rid of.

Intestinal gas

One of the bacteria's by-products is gas. Inside your body, this gas is called intestinal gas. It mixes with other gases that have been swallowed into your digestive system. To avoid blowing up like a balloon, your body needs to get rid of this gas. In fact, on average people need to get rid of about 170 ounces (0.5 L) of gas every day.

As it leaves your body, the gas changes its name to "wind" (or **flatulence**). Wind is usually about 58% nitrogen, 21% hydrogen, 9% carbon dioxide, 7% methane, and 4% oxygen. The remaining 1% contains sulfur—which is usually what makes it smell.

Tiny, gas-producing bacteria are hard at work in a large intestine.

STRANGE BUT TRUE!

In France, a performer called Le Pétomane was popular before World War I. Le Pétomane is French for "The Fartomaniac." His act involved playing instruments, blowing out candles, and even blasting out songs—using wind from his bottom.

Breaking wind

Many people claim never to break wind, but everyone does to release the gas that builds up in their intestines. Most of the time the gas passes out in small quantities and doesn't smell—so you don't notice. When it does smell, or there is more of it, it is probably to do with what you have eaten.

Whatever they tell you—EVERYONE breaks wind.

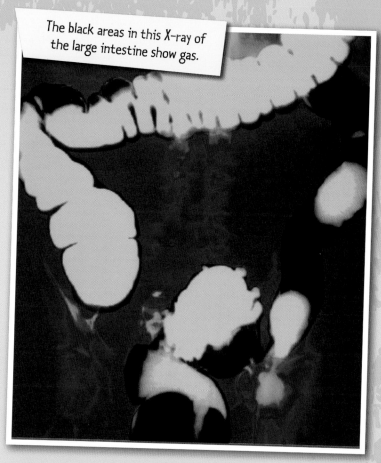

The black areas in this X-ray of the large intestine show gas.

See for yourself

NOTE: Do NOT do this experiment if you are likely to be in a confined space with other people.*

The food you eat affects the smell of your wind. Food containing sulfur will make it smell worse, because of the gas produced by sulfur-seeking bacteria. These foods include beans, onions, cabbage, cheese, and eggs. Try some, and see what happens.

*Handy hint: Your wind can be smelt 10-15 seconds after release. That gives you plenty of time to move away, or claim that the dog did it.

DON'T TRY THIS AT HOME!

An ancient Roman emperor named Claudius (10BCE–54CE) passed a law saying that breaking wind was allowed at banquets. Claudius thought holding it in was bad for you. (Even today, doctors don't agree on whether he was correct or not.)

More recently, in 2011 Malawi's Minister of Justice suggested that breaking wind in public should be made illegal. People found the idea so funny he had to withdraw it.

DIGESTIVE WASTE: STOOLS

Your body is good at getting the maximum possible nutrition from your food. By the time it reaches the end of the long intestine, all that's left are things your body does not need. This has formed into solid lumps called stool—which lots of people call poop.

How fast is your digestion?

The answer is different from person to person. It depends on the kind of food you eat. People whose food contains a lot of fiber usually digest it quicker. If your food is short on fiber, it takes longer to pass through. On average, food takes twice as long to be processed in wealthy countries, where people eat less fiber.

DID YOU KNOW?

In ancient Rome, not everyone had their own toilet.

Many people used public ones. These were very sociable—there were no walls, so you could sit and chat to your neighbor!

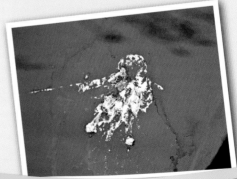

STRANGE BUT TRUE!

Bird poop is partly white because birds can't urinate. Instead, their bodies mix poop (the black part) and urine-sludge (the white part) together.

Questions answered

People often have lots of questions about poop, but are embarrassed about asking them. So here are some answers!

How often should you go? There is no correct answer to this question, because everyone is different. However, as long as you normally go between three times a day and four times a week, you are in the normal range.

What makes stools smell? The blame lies with the same bacteria that make your wind smell. As they break down food, the bacteria produce by-products, some of which stay in your stool.

Why are stools brown? Stool gets its color from the red **pigment** in red blood cells called **bilirubin**. When red blood cells die, a lot of the pigment they contained ends up in your intestines—and then in your stool.

What your stool says about you

You can learn a lot from your stool. The shape, size, and color all give clues about your diet and digestion. In fact, there is even an international chart to help analyze stool, called the Bristol Stool Chart. Number Types 3 and 4 are the healthiest!

DON'T TRY THIS AT HOME!

Constipation is the name for when you need to let out some stool, but can't. It can be painful and upsetting, but today it is easily cured with medication or other treatments. Things were not always that way—crazy constipation cures from the past included:

* squirting yogurt up someone's bottom;
* swallowing mercury (a liquid that is actually poisonous);
* squirting water, perfume, and herbs up someone's bottom (King Louis XIV of France apparently had this done four times a day!).

BRISTOL STOOL CHART

TYPE 1		Separate hard lumps, like nuts (hard to pass)
TYPE 2		Sausage-shaped but lumpy
TYPE 3		Like a sausage but with cracks on its surface
TYPE 4		Like a sausage or snake, smooth and soft
TYPE 5		Soft blobs with clear-cut edges (passed easily)
TYPE 6		Fluffy pieces with ragged edges, a mushy stool
TYPE 7		Watery, no solid pieces-entirely liquid

PROCESSING LIQUIDS

To stay alive, you need to drink fluid as well as eat food. In fact, although most food is mainly made up of water, some would claim drinking is more important than eating. You can stay alive for weeks without food—but only a few days without fluid.

adult's bladder is about the size of a pear. As it fills with urine, it expands. A full bladder can be the size of a small melon!

When your body senses that your bladder is full, your brain receives a message saying it's time to go to the restroom. When you get there, muscles in your bladder relax, two valves open, and the urine flows out.

Fluid's jobs in your body

The water your body gets from drinking and processing food is important. Water makes up the biggest part of your blood, helps your joints to move, and is essential for keeping your brain working properly. Your body also uses water to flush away waste products.

The kidneys and bladder

Waste products are cleaned out of your blood by your kidneys. You have two kidneys. They combine the waste with water, making urine. The urine passes down two tubes called **ureters** to your bladder. When empty, an

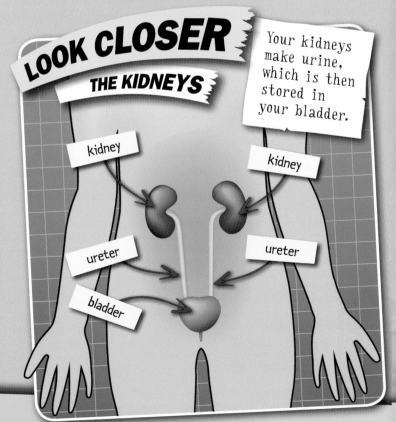

LOOK CLOSER
THE KIDNEYS

Your kidneys make urine, which is then stored in your bladder.

kidney

kidney

ureter

ureter

bladder

What your urine says about you

It used to be common for doctors to sniff, or even SIP, patients' urine as a way of figuring out what was wrong with them. So, what can your urine reveal about you?

① Color

Normally, urine should be a pale yellow color. If it gets darker, this shows that it contains more waste products and less water. So dark yellow urine probably means you are not drinking enough.

② Smell

Urine does not normally smell strongly. If your urine smells sweet, or like bleach, it may be a sign that you should visit the doctor. (Although If you have been eating asparagus, wait a day. Asparagus makes most people's urine smell strange.)

Urine can be used to test for health problems.

DON'T TRY THIS AT HOME!

In ancient Rome, people rubbed urine into their teeth to make them whiter. Urine contains a chemical called ammonia, which DOES bleach the color out of things—so this treatment should actually work! Today, though, there are much more pleasant ways to whiten teeth.

STRANGE BUT TRUE!

rhubarb

beets

Some foods can affect the color of some people's urine—but this isn't true for everyone. Some people might experience the following:

✳ reddish urine from eating lots of beets;

✳ dark brown, or even black urine, from eating fava beans or rhubarb;

✳ pink urine from eating blackberries.

blackberries

VOMIT AND OTHER PROBLEMS

Sometimes, your digestive system has a problem and wants to get rid of its contents fast. When this happens, there are only two possible escape routes: coming back up or out the bottom.

The norovirus is also called the "vomiting bug!"

Vomiting

If your body detects something in your food that's bad for you, you may have to vomit. People also vomit for other reasons, including eating too much, feeling very scared, **motion sickness**, and illness caused by harmful microbes such as viruses or bacteria. Whatever the cause, you don't usually have much choice over when you vomit. When you vomit, an emergency message from your brain tells the muscles in your digestive system to go into reverse. Instead of pushing food down, they force it rapidly up to your mouth— and out.

Diarrhea

If something upsets your large intestine, it also gets rid of its contents—often very quickly. This sudden urge to sit down on a toilet and go is called diarrhea.

YOU CAN'T TRY THIS AT HOME!

In 1969, Neil Armstrong and Buzz Aldrin became the first humans ever to set foot on the Moon. Like typical tourists they left a few things behind when they went home, including footprints that are still there today and an American flag on a pole. They also left behind a bag of vomit, caused by space sickness.

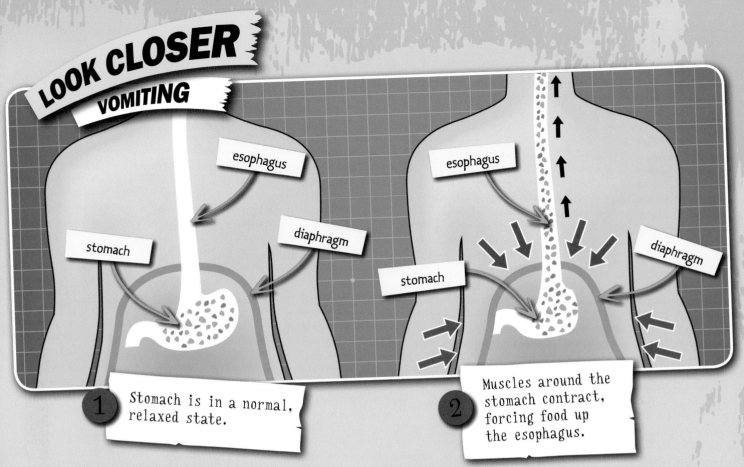

esophagus

stomach

diaphragm

esophagus

stomach

diaphragm

1 Stomach is in a normal, relaxed state.

2 Muscles around the stomach contract, forcing food up the esophagus.

A virus is usually responsible, but diarrhea also happens if food you have eaten contains poisonous bacteria. Your body senses the problem and acts quickly to get rid of it.

When you have diarrhea, your body speeds up the process of getting rid of your stool. To do this, it increases peristalsis in the large intestine. The water that would usually be absorbed here is rushed on, making your stool watery and soft. Then the muscles of your large intestine contract to force the stool out.

DID YOU KNOW?

Ancient Rome had vomitoriums.

Ancient Romans are said to have had "vomitoriums." These are believed to have been rooms where people at a feast could go to vomit up what they'd eaten and drunk. Then the vomiters could go back and carry on with the party.

The "vomitorium" DID exist—but it was actually a kind of large passageway in a theater or amphitheater which allowed lots of people to arrive or leave quickly.

STRANGE BUT TRUE!

Sperm whale vomit and stool sometimes contain a valuable substance called ambergris, which was once used in making perfumes.

Only about 1% of sperm whales produce ambergris, and very little of what is released is ever found. It's not surprising that perfume makers have now found alternative materials!

MAINTENANCE AND SERVICING

People eat all sorts of different foods. Strange snacks from around the world include fried spiders in Cambodia, lime-and-garlic grasshoppers in Mexico, and even rotten sharks in Iceland. Our amazing digestive systems can cope with them all!

small enough to swallow. Unfortunately, your mouth is full of bacteria, which eat the little bits of food that get left behind. As they do this, the bacteria release **plaque** on to your teeth. Unless it is regularly brushed off, the plaque eats away at the teeth and eventually destroys them.

Digestive troubles

Even though your digestive system can cope with spicy spiders or fried grasshoppers, it is not indestructible. If you eat the wrong foods or are sick, your digestive system can stop working properly. The most common problems include pain in your abdomen, constipation, and diarrhea. So, what are the best ways to keep everything digesting properly?

 ## See for yourself

Before you brush your teeth in the morning, scrape them with your nail. Have a look at the white stuff that has been scraped off—that's tooth-attacking plaque. Imagine how much would build up if you didn't brush your teeth for 24 hours.

Brush your teeth

Your teeth are the first stage of digestion. You need them to mash your food into pieces

A BALANCED DIET

Plenty of fruits and vegetables! These contain vitamins and **minerals**, which are vital for health, and also provide fiber.

Plenty of foods such as bread, rice, potatoes, and pasta. These provide **carbohydrates** (which your body uses for energy) and nutrients.

Some milk and dairy foods such as cheese or yogurt. These provide protein, which your body uses for growth and repair work, and calcium to keep your bones and teeth strong.

Some meat, fish, eggs, and beans, which contain protein, vitamins, and minerals.

Small amounts (if any) of cake, candy, and soda.

Eat a healthy diet

This is important for two reasons. First, a healthy diet will help keep your digestive system working properly. Second, a healthy diet contains all the nutrients you need for your body to grow and work properly.

Drink, drink, drink

Water is important in the digestive system. People should try to drink about half a gallon (1.9 L) of fluid every day to keep everything working properly. Exactly how much you need to drink depends on how big you are and what you eat. This is because you also get fluid from the food you eat.

DID YOU KNOW?

Drinking fruit juice and brushing your teeth don't mix.

You should avoid drinking fruit juice if you are about to brush your teeth. The citric acid in fruit juice weakens your teeth's protective coating for about half an hour. If you brush your teeth in that time, you will be brushing away the teeth's protection!

GUTSY WORDS!

Note: Some boldfaced words are defined where they appear in the book.

abdomen The part of the body containing your digestive organs, basically from the bottom of your ribs to your hips

absorb To soak up or take in

bacteria Tiny living organisms made up of a single cell. Bacteria in your body do lots of useful jobs, particularly in digesting food, but some types of bacteria can also cause illness.

blood vessels Tubes that carry blood around the body

bolus A ball of chewed food and saliva that is swallowed when you eat

byproduct Something that is produced as a side effect, for example, when you boil water, you also get steam

carbohydrates Types of sugars that the body uses for energy that are found in some foods

circulatory system The system that moves blood around the body, made up of blood vessels and organs such as the heart

contract To shorten

enzymes Chemicals that make a process inside your body happen, or happen more quickly. In your digestive system, enzymes are important for breaking food down so that your body can use it.

lubricant usually a liquid or semi-liquid that makes it easier for one object to slide past another

membrane A thin, flexible layer that usually makes up part of a a cell, tissue, or organ

microbe A microorganism that exists as just one cell, and can only be seen with a microscope

mineral A non-living natural substance, for example iron. Your body needs certain minerals to stay healthy.

motion sickness The feeling that you are about to be sick, or actually being sick, as a result of movement

mucus A protective coating and lubricant produced in various parts of your body

nasal passages The airways that connect your nostrils to your throat

nutrients Substances in food that are used by the body to keep working and for growth and repair

peristalsis The squeezing movement made by muscles to move food through parts of the digestive system, such as the esophagus and the small intestine

pigment A type of natural coloring found in animal or plant tissue

plaque A layer of mucus and bacteria found on the teeth that can cause cavities

valve A structure in an organ with a flap to allow one-way flow of fluid through it

virus A tiny living organism that lives inside the cells of other organisms, and can cause diseases

vitamin A kind of nutrient, needed in very small amounts for your body to work properly and grow

DIGEST THIS INFORMATION

Are you hungry for extra information about your digestive system? Here are some good places to find out more:

BOOKS TO READ

Burnstein, John. *The Dynamic Digestive System: How does my stomach work?* Crabtree Publishing, 2009.

Claybourne, Anna. *Smelly Farts and Other Body Horrors*. Crabtree Publishing, 2015.

Shea, John. *The Digestive System*. Gareth Stevens, 2012.

Sohn, Emily. *A Journey through the Digestive System with Max Axiom, Super Scientist*. Capstone Press, 2009.

WEBSITES

http://kidshealth.org/kid/htbw/digestive_system.html

This website is a really good place to find out all sorts of information about the human body. It has an excellent section on the digestive system.

www.neok12.com/Digestive-System.htm

This website has all sorts of information for kids on how the digestive system works, including diagrams, videos, and quizzes.

PLACES TO VISIT

In Boston, Massachusetts, the **Hall of Human Life** at the **Museum of Science** has over 70 interactive exhibits about how the body works. The museum is located at:

Museum of Science
1 Science Park
Boston, MA 02114
www.mos.org

The **Museum of Science and Industry** in Chicago, Illinois, features YOU! The Experience, a permanent exhibition celebrating human life.
The museum is located at:

The Museum of Science and Industry
5700 S. Lake Shore Drive
Chicago, IL 60637
www.msichicago.org

In Columbus, Ohio, the **Center of Science and Industry** explores the human body in their exhibition Life: The Story of You. The museum is located at:

Center for Science and Industry
333 W. Broad Street
Columbus, OH 43215
www.cosi.org

INDEX

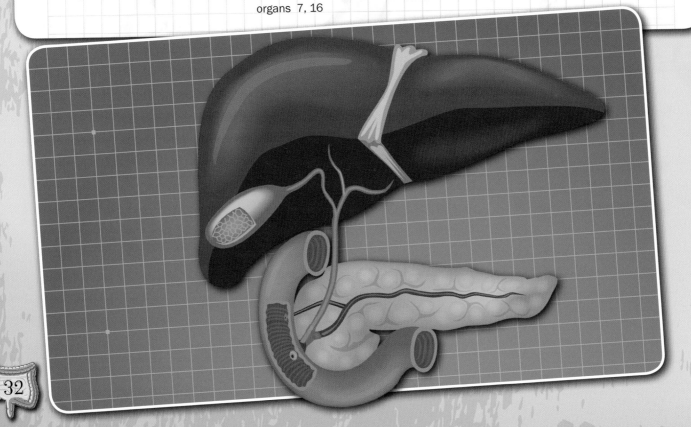